TONY PAYNE AND
GEOFF ROBSON

THE
GENEROSITY
PROJECT

LEARN, PRAY AND WORK TOGETHER
TO BECOME THE BIG-HEARTED PEOPLE
GOD CALLS US TO BE

SYDNEY · YOUNGSTOWN

Matthias Media
(St Matthias Press Ltd ACN 067 558 365)
Email: info@matthiasmedia.com.au
Internet: www.matthiasmedia.com.au
Please visit our website for current postal and telephone contact information.

Matthias Media (USA)
Email: sales@matthiasmedia.com
Internet: www.matthiasmedia.com
Please visit our website for current postal and telephone contact information.

ISBN 978 1 925424 57 7

Cover design and typesetting by Lankshear Design.

Contents

About *The Generosity Project*

Generosity. Our culture prizes it, and our churches proclaim it. Our lives are better for it, whether we're givers or receivers.

Yet as much as we believe in generosity, we're painfully aware of the powerful lure of greed—in our world, and in our own hearts. Should we look outside ourselves and be generous, or should we look out for ourselves and let the chips fall where they may? We feel this tension, and know that we often fail.

As God's people, we need to pause and listen carefully to what God says to us about generosity. More than that, we need to change—to repent of our selfishness, and to encourage each other to lead generous lives that reflect God's incredible generosity to us.

The Generosity Project aims to help us do just that. It's a 'project' because it's not meant to be a book that we read on our own, but an ongoing task to engage in with others—where we help each other learn and understand what God is saying about generosity, and then pray for and encourage one other to put it into practice.

So *The Generosity Project* is not designed around an individual reader—it's a framework of content to work through with at least one other person, or with a small group of others.

Apart from part 1 (which has an extra introduction), the six parts of *The Generosity Project* all have three main sections:

a. a Bible study section, with passages to read and discuss together (this should take around 20-25 minutes)

b. input that draws the various strands of the Bible's teaching together (you can watch this input via a free online video, featuring Bible teachers from the UK and Australia; or you can pause and read the text version that is supplied, either silently or out loud; either way, the input section will take 10-15 minutes)

c. questions and case studies to help you discuss and pray about what you've learned, and to apply it to your own lives (this can take 15-20 minutes, or as much time as you want to give it!).

Everything you need to work on *The Generosity Project* is in this book or online at thegenerosityproject.com.

On the website you'll find:

- links for ordering more copies of this book (each person who is taking part will need one)
- seven free videos for the 'Input' sections
- additional free 'Real world stories' videos, giving case studies of generosity in action
- a free downloadable guide for group leaders
- a free downloadable guide for church leaders to help you implement *The Generosity Project* throughout your church—not just as a program for small groups but as part of a wider effort to change the culture of generosity in your church community.

Our thanks to the many people whose hard work and generosity have made this book and the supporting videos and website possible. We are especially grateful to:

- Simon Pillar and the working group he assembled to initiate and drive the project (Richard Borgonon, Jeremy Marshall, Simon Pilcher, Ben Stone and Nicholas Bewes)
- the five Bible teachers who gave so warmly of their time and experience for the input sections (see details on page 9)
- the many people who spoke to us on the street about generosity, or who told us their real world stories of generosity
- David and Ash Tucker from ShowReal, who did such a brilliant job on the videos

- the team at Matthias Media for editing, designing and publishing this book, and for building the website.

With trust in the generous God who makes everything possible, we pray that the result of all of our efforts will be a new spirit of generosity in your heart, and a new culture of generosity that permeates the life of your church.

Contributors

In the second half of 2018, we enlisted the help of five respected Bible teachers from the UK and Australia to help us sharpen and articulate the key ideas of *The Generosity Project*. You'll see them appearing regularly in the 'Input' sections, whether talking in the videos or being quoted in the sections of text. The five contributors are (in alphabetical order):

 Tim Clemens, Lead Pastor at Grace City Church, Waterloo, in Sydney

 John Stevens, National Director of the Fellowship of Independent Evangelical Churches (UK)

 Jason Roach, Senior Minister at The Bridge (Battersea Community Church) in London

 Dan Wu, Old Testament Lecturer at Moore Theological College in Newtown

 Vaughan Roberts, Rector of St Ebbe's Church in Oxford

PART 1: A world built on generosity

Introducing *The Generosity Project*

(Watch video 1a or read the following.)

If you stand on a busy street corner or in a park—as I did while preparing to write this book—and ask random passers-by what they think about 'generosity', a couple of things strike you pretty quickly.

Firstly, American tourists are very generous in giving their time to talk about generosity, certainly more than Aussies. And as for Brits, let's just say that getting them to stop and talk on camera is about as easy as finding a public loo in central London.

But among those who did stop and talk, a common view about 'generosity' rose rapidly to the surface.

"Generosity is giving back; giving to others."

"It's giving of yourself without questioning it, and without thinking of your own needs."

"It's doing things for other people that you don't get a reward for."

And from an English woman, perhaps the best definition of all: "I think it's the willingness to give up any of your own resources, whether that be time, money or just advice, to help other people who are in need or who have asked for your help".

Generosity is not that hard to understand. It's giving someone more than is expected, like a generous helping of ice-cream. Or it's kindly giving someone more than you're obliged to, like stopping to talk to a random stranger on the street about generosity when you have other places to be.

But while generosity may be straightforward enough as a concept, it's anything but straightforward to display. It's much easier to describe a generous person than to be one.

A well-known social science experiment in the 1970s illustrated the problem. Some theological college students were asked to prepare a short talk on the parable of the Good Samaritan. When they arrived at class, they were told that they needed to go to another building on campus to deliver their talks. Some were told that their audience was already waiting for them, and that they had no time to lose.

On their way to deliver their talks, the students came upon an actor who was slumped on the footpath, moaning and pretending to be in distress.

You can guess what happened.

Only 53% of the students hurrying to give talks on a famous parable about generosity stopped to help the man. And the variable that had the most effect on whether they stopped or not was how much time pressure they thought they were under to get to the building to deliver their talks.[1]

It's easy to approve of generosity, but much more difficult to be generous.

Perhaps this is why we find generosity difficult even to talk about. Vaughan Roberts, Rector of St Ebbe's Church, Oxford, says that in many churches, generosity is the great unmentionable:

> **We don't tend to talk about money. We don't tend to talk about giving. And I'd love to break that taboo, because the Bible is not embarrassed about these things and nor should we be.[2]**

In many ways, if *The Generosity Project* achieves nothing else but this—to get Christians thinking and praying and talking honestly about generosity—it will have provided a valuable service.

---

1 John M Darley and C Daniel Batson, '"From Jerusalem to Jericho": A study of situational and dispositional variables in helping behavior', *Journal of Personality and Social Psychology*, vol. 27, no. 1, July 1973, pp. 100-8.

2 The quotes from pastor-teachers like Vaughan Roberts that appear throughout *The Generosity Project* are taken from interviews conducted in late 2018 and early 2019. The five Bible teachers we interviewed are listed on page 9.

Of course, an awkwardness or unwillingness to talk about generosity is not our only problem. According to UK Fellowship of Independent Evangelical Churches (FIEC) Director John Stevens, one very significant issue is that many Christians don't realize how much capacity they have to be generous:

> I think one issue we have in our culture is that many people don't actually feel very wealthy, and so life feels pressured. They are trying to pay their mortgage, pay for their cars, care for their children. Although in objective terms, in the light of history and the world as it is today, they are remarkably wealthy, I don't think many people *feel* wealthy. And therefore they don't feel like they have got much they could give.

Then there are the questions that many of us have about generosity:

- How much should we give away, and what is legitimate to keep and use for our own needs?
- What about being generous with our time and abilities—does that count as generosity?
- Where should we direct our generosity when there are so many needs in the world—not only at church and for the spread of the gospel but in the physical suffering and hardship that is so widespread?

And, of course, there is the biggest obstacle of all to generosity: the constant tendency of our hearts to lean away from generosity and towards selfishness. We can't talk about generosity without also talking about its counterpart and enemy: the greed that wants to *get* rather than to *give*.

The purpose of *The Generosity Project* should now be clear.

It's to help Christians and churches learn about generosity—what motivates and increases it, what blocks and shrivels it, what it might look like in our lives and churches, and where and how we can practise it. But more than this, the goal is to help you learn to *live a radically generous life* in response to the incredible generosity of God, and to do that as part of a radically generous church community in which we can encourage each other to be generous, and work together in generosity to others.

That's why this is a 'project' and not just a book to read. Our prayer is that, as you are confronted by what God says about generosity in the Bible, and reflect on those truths (hopefully in conversation with others), the result will be what God always achieves through his word—the transformation of his people to be more like his Son, the one who "though he was rich, yet for your sake he became poor, so that you by his poverty might become rich" (2 Cor 8:9).

Read and reflect: Understanding God and his world

1. What comes to mind for you when you hear the word 'generosity'? Can you think of an example of someone that you regard as being truly generous? What makes this person generous?

2. What questions about generosity would you like to have answered by the end of this course?

3. Read the following Bible passages. What do you learn in each one about God and his creation?

   a. 1 Chronicles 29:10-14

   [10] Therefore David blessed the LORD in the presence of all the assembly. And David said: "Blessed are you, O LORD, the God of Israel our father, forever and ever. [11] Yours, O LORD, is the greatness and the power and the glory and the victory and the majesty, for all that is in the heavens and in the earth is yours. Yours is the kingdom, O LORD, and you are exalted as head above all. [12] Both riches and honour come from you, and you rule over all. In your hand are power and might, and in your hand it is to make great and to give strength to all. [13] And now we thank you, our God, and praise your glorious name.

   [14] "But who am I, and what is my people, that we should be able thus to offer willingly? For all things come from you, and of your own have we given you."

b. Psalm 95:3-6

> [3] For the Lord is a great God,
>   and a great King above all gods.
> [4] In his hand are the depths of the earth;
>   the heights of the mountains are his also.
> [5] The sea is his, for he made it,
>   and his hands formed the dry land.
>
> [6] Oh come, let us worship and bow down;
>   let us kneel before the Lord, our Maker!

4. What do the following two passages say about how God *continues* to relate to his creation?

a. Psalm 104:24-30

> [24] O Lord, how manifold are your works!
>   In wisdom have you made them all;
>   the earth is full of your creatures.
> [25] Here is the sea, great and wide,
>   which teems with creatures innumerable,
>   living things both small and great.
> [26] There go the ships,
>   and Leviathan, which you formed to play in it.

^{27} These all look to you,
  to give them their food in due season.
^{28} When you give it to them, they gather it up;
  when you open your hand, they are filled
    with good things.
^{29} When you hide your face, they are dismayed;
  when you take away their breath, they die
    and return to their dust.
^{30} When you send forth your Spirit, they are
    created,
  and you renew the face of the ground.

b. Acts 17:24-28

^{24} "The God who made the world and everything
in it, being Lord of heaven and earth, does not
live in temples made by man, ^{25} nor is he served
by human hands, as though he needed anything,
since he himself gives to all mankind life and
breath and everything. ^{26} And he made from one
man every nation of mankind to live on all the
face of the earth, having determined allotted
periods and the boundaries of their dwelling

place, [27] that they should seek God, and perhaps feel their way toward him and find him. Yet he is actually not far from each one of us, [28] for

"'In him we live and move and have our being';

as even some of your own poets have said,

"'For we are indeed his offspring.'"

5. How do you think we should *respond* to God as the generous Creator and Sustainer of the world? (The passages you've already read cast some light on this.)

Input: God, the generous Creator and Sustainer

(Watch video 1b or read the following.)

When Bart Simpson is asked to say grace, he says, "Dear God, we paid for all this stuff ourselves, so thanks for nothing. Amen."[3]

The watching adults gasp. Mr Burns chuckles and says, "Only an innocent child could get away with such blasphemy. God bless them all."

But Bart's caustic honesty is funny because, as comedy so often does, it pierces through the veneer of polite sentiment and says aloud what many of the watching adults are actually thinking anyway.

We did go to work. We did earn the money. We did pay for this stuff ourselves. So why all the thanksgiving to a God we can't see?

The Bible's answer is that the God we can't see created everything we can see and touch and hear and feel, including us. He created the molecules that make up our bodies. He gave life and breath to those bodies that go to work to earn money. He provided the power and ability to work, the materials to work with, and the world within which that work is effective and productive and satisfying. He created the plants and animals that we buy as food with our hard-earned money, and the land and the rain and the sun that sustain and grow them. He made

3   *The Simpsons,* television program, season 2, episode 4.

and organized everything and everyone that constructed the house in which we sit to eat the food, the kitchen in which it was prepared, the table and plate it rests on.

All this is obvious enough if we open our eyes and see it.

Senior Minister Jason Roach, who was a surgeon before he became a pastor, puts it like this:

> I used to be in medical practice. On the operating table, you'd get to see hearts beating time after time after time. You'd be bowled over by the fact that God is the generous Creator and Provider. More than that, I thought about how our tongues work, and how God provided taste buds with sweet and sour and all kinds of different things. You realize this is a God who hasn't just provided food for us to eat that satisfies us and fills our bellies, but a God who gives us all kinds of food to delight in.

All that we are and have and do comes from an infinitely powerful and loving Creator—from One who is so much above and beyond us that we can barely comprehend his greatness, but One who is loving and generous, and showers us with more than we can ask or imagine. God doesn't have to do any of this. He is not obligated to create or sustain us. It is not something we have earned or deserved. God creates and sustains and provides simply because of who he is, out of his character of love and faithfulness. And this is really the essence of generosity: to give abundantly beyond any expectation or obligation.

The poetry of the psalms often expresses the greatness of God as generous Creator and Provider, along with how we should respond to him. In Psalm 95, for example:

> Oh come, let us sing to the LORD;
> > let us make a joyful noise to the rock of our
> > > salvation!
> Let us come into his presence with thanksgiving;
> > let us make a joyful noise to him with songs
> > > of praise!
> For the LORD is a great God,
> > and a great King above all gods.
> In his hand are the depths of the earth;
> > the heights of the mountains are his also.
> The sea is his, for he made it,
> > and his hands formed the dry land.
>
> Oh come, let us worship and bow down;
> > let us kneel before the LORD, our Maker!
> > > (Ps 95:1-6)

With raucous celebration and thanksgiving on one hand and humble recognition of our place as creatures on the other, the psalmist calls on Israel to recognize and respond to their supremely powerful Maker.

This is the right and basic response to God's generosity as Creator and Sustainer of all things—not that we're all that good at making this response. Vaughan Roberts says:

> God delights when we enjoy the rich variety and wonder of the world that he's made. He gives us so much more than we need and so much more than we deserve. God is the giver, and we are the takers. So we take and take and take, but hardly ever stop and say those little words: 'Thank you'. I think most of us, certainly those of us who call ourselves Christians, know very well that God is the great giver, but it's very easy to forget it and live with the illusion of control—as though somehow we are in control of our lives and that we've earned the things we get through our own efforts. We take them for granted. We don't stop to say 'Thank you'. It's ridiculous, because when we stop to think, surely we realize everything we have is a gift of God's amazing grace. He is the definition of generosity.

In this sense, Bart Simpson's declaration of self-sufficiency—we did this ourselves, so why be thankful to God?—is the limited perspective of a child, like the clench-fisted toddler who insists he can do everything *himself*. The toddler doesn't see the larger perspective: that his parents provide *everything* for him, that he is utterly dependent on them, and that there is almost nothing that he can actually do by himself.

Romans 1 says that this is in fact the basic attitude of *all humanity*—a refusal to respond to the obvious truth that God has created and given us everything. Humanity refuses to honour God or give thanks to him as Creator, but turns its honour and love towards created things instead (Rom 1:18-23).

We'll think further about humanity's negative response to God's generosity in part 2—particularly as it manifests itself in greed—but let's stay positive for the moment. What are the positive implications and responses to God's outlandish generosity to us as his creatures?

Grace City Church Pastor Tim Clemens puts it this way:

> Once you see that God didn't have to create us but has generously chosen to create us, and that he is both willing and able to provide for us in an ongoing way... it just changes everything.
>
> So to begin with, it lays a foundation of contentment because now I can have confidence that everything I have is what God intended. If he wanted me to have more, he could have given it to me. He's certainly able to. And so I'm now left in a place where I can rejoice and give thanks to God for what I do have, rather than murmuring about all the things that I don't have.
>
> But then on top of that, understanding how generous God has been to me in creation helps me to become a more generous person, because now I can operate out of faith rather than fear. I don't have to be anxious and fearful about what might happen in the future. Instead, I can have faith, trusting that the same God who so generously provided for me and us in creation will continue to provide for me all of my needs into the future, right into eternity. And that frees me to be generous towards others with all that I have.

> 'Generosity' is a funny word in church circles. It's often the word that we use when we actually are trying to talk about money. Generosity is about more than money, but it's not about less than money, because money is really a liquid form of God's good and generous gift to us in creation.

Tim is right, and we'll need to talk about money at some point in our thinking about generosity, but now is not that time. For now, we need to pause and reflect on what it means that everything in our lives and our world is built on generosity—the generosity of the Creator—and that the right response to God's generosity is thanksgiving, contentment, trust and a generosity of our own.

What it means for us

(Talk about one or more of the following questions together.)

1. What insight from the 'Input' section struck you most? Why?

2. Do you have an example to share of God's generosity to you? How did your awareness of God's provision affect you? How did you respond?

3. When do you find it hard to remember your complete dependence on God? What practical steps can you take to increase your thankfulness for God's provision and your awareness of how much you rely on him?

4. When are you most tempted to be anxious about your earthly needs? How can the truths we've seen in part 1 help you manage this anxiety?

5. Think of as many examples as you can of wrong or poor responses to God's generosity.

Take some time to give thanks to God for his generosity towards you. Give thanks for specific examples of his goodness.

Going further

If you haven't done so already, read the text or watch the video in the 'Input' section (above) sometime over the next few days. It will help solidify the ideas in your mind, as you continue to think and pray about generosity.

PART 2: The inward curve of the heart

We finished part 1 by thinking about how good and generous God is, and about how we should respond to his generosity—with thanksgiving, with trust and contentment, and with an openhearted generosity of our own.

But we find this hard, of course. Somehow, it's easier to grumble than to give thanks, to fret about finances than to trust God's generosity, to spend our resources on ourselves rather than generously sharing them with others.

And it's not just money. We often find it just as hard, if not more so, to be generous with our time, or our homes, or our gifts, or our other resources. In all kinds of ways, we may want to be generous, but our weaknesses and failings draw us away from being the generous people we know God wants us to be in response to his infinite generosity to us.

Why are we like this?

Read and reflect: What's wrong with us?

1. Read the following passage from Romans:

    [18] For the wrath of God is revealed from heaven against all ungodliness and unrighteousness of men, who by their unrighteousness suppress the truth. [19] For what can be known about God is plain to them, because God has shown it to them. [20] For his invisible attributes, namely, his eternal power and divine nature, have been clearly perceived, ever since the creation of the world, in the things that have been made. So they are without excuse. [21] For although they knew God, they did not honour him as God or give thanks to him, but they became futile in their thinking, and their foolish hearts were darkened. [22] Claiming to be wise, they became fools, [23] and exchanged the glory of the immortal God for images resembling mortal man and birds and animals and creeping things.

    [24] Therefore God gave them up in the lusts of their hearts to impurity, to the dishonouring of their bodies among themselves, [25] because they exchanged the truth about God for a lie and worshipped and served the creature rather than the Creator, who is blessed forever! Amen. (Rom 1:18-25)

a. How does this passage describe the classic human response to God?

b. How does this passage describe the consequences of the way humans treat God?

c. Based on this passage, how would you summarize in your own words what's wrong with humanity?

2. Read the following passage from Deuteronomy, where God is warning Israel (through Moses) about the dangers of wealth:

[11] "Take care lest you forget the LORD your God by not keeping his commandments and his rules and his statutes, which I command you today, [12] lest, when you have eaten and are full and have built good houses and live in them, [13] and when your herds and flocks multiply and your silver and gold is multiplied and all that you have is multiplied, [14] then your heart be lifted up, and you forget the LORD your God, who brought you out of the land of Egypt, out of the house of slavery, [15] who led you through the great and terrifying wilderness, with its fiery serpents and scorpions and thirsty ground where there was no water, who brought you water out of the flinty rock, [16] who fed you in the wilderness with manna that your fathers did not know, that he might humble you and test you, to do you good in the end. [17] Beware lest you say in your heart, 'My power and the might of my hand have gotten me this wealth.' [18] You shall remember the LORD your God, for it is he who gives you power to get wealth, that he may confirm his covenant that he swore to your fathers, as it is this day. [19] And if you forget the LORD your God and go after other gods and serve them and worship them,

I solemnly warn you today that you shall surely perish. ²⁰ Like the nations that the Lord makes to perish before you, so shall you perish, because you would not obey the voice of the Lord your God." (Deut 8:11-20)

a. What danger did wealth present to the Israelites?

b. Do you think our attitude to money can reveal our heart attitude to God? If so, how?

3. Now read the following passage from Ephesians to see what God does about our problem:

[1] And you were dead in the trespasses and sins [2] in which you once walked, following the course of this world, following the prince of the power of the air, the spirit that is now at work in the sons of disobedience—[3] among whom we all once lived in the passions of our flesh, carrying out the desires of the body and the mind, and were by nature children of wrath, like the rest of mankind. [4] But God, being rich in mercy, because of the great love with which he loved us, [5] even when we were dead in our trespasses, made us alive together with Christ—by grace you have been saved—[6] and raised us up with him and seated us with him in the heavenly places in Christ Jesus, [7] so that in the coming ages he might show the immeasurable riches of his grace in kindness toward us in Christ Jesus. [8] For by grace you have been saved through faith. And this is not your own doing; it is the gift of God, [9] not a result of works, so that no-one may boast. [10] For we are his workmanship, created in Christ Jesus for good works, which God prepared beforehand, that we should walk in them. (Eph 2:1-10)

What does this extraordinary passage teach us about:

a. the real nature of our problem?

b. what God has done about this problem?

c. what motivates this amazing action of God?

d. what our response should be?

Input: Our heart problem and God's solution

(Watch video 2 or read the following.)

In January 2008, Manoj Raithatha's life was a picture postcard of material and family success. From small beginnings he had built a property investment company that owned whole blocks of apartments across the UK. He had it all: a devoted wife, children in private schools, big house, expensive car, and the money to spend on lavish holidays and expensive clothes.

But all was not well. Manoj puts it like this:

> My success changed me as a person very, very radically. I became ruthless. I became arrogant. And friendships didn't really matter any more. So there were a lot of friendships that I had, but money changed me so much that money was more important than people—and so people got sidelined and the draw of money just kept on, kept on luring me to make more money.
>
> Was I happy? No. I liken it to the idea of going up to the top of a mountain. And what do you expect to see at the top of a mountain? You expect to see some beautiful scenery, a sense of 'I have arrived', a sense of satisfaction, contentment, but it was never there. We got to the top of a mountain after doing one deal and we were never happy, and so essentially, I would try and do another deal to get happier. But money just didn't bring me any joy whatsoever.

> 2008 was going to be a massive year for the company. We had bought some 900 apartments across the UK. But we all know what happened in 2008. The financial market collapsed.

Manoj's company became almost worthless overnight. 2008 also brought a crisis in the health of his son, who was a severe asthmatic:

> In February 2008, just before the crash happened, my son was ill again, and I got a phone call from my wife who was in the ambulance. She phoned me to say that I needed to rush and get to the hospital quickly. I knew the drill, but after three rounds of the nebulizer and that failing to work we were rushed into resuscitation with my son. And I remember to this day, vividly remember holding my son; and his airways shut down and he stopped breathing. But I found myself in that moment, collapsing to my knees in prayer along with my wife, because there was nowhere I could go.
>
> My son ended up in St Thomas's in London; he was transferred to the hospital. Basically he was in an induced coma as they tried to work out what was going on and the consultant spoke to us on the fourth day and said, "I am really sorry but your son is not going to open his eyes for some time yet".[1]

---

1   Manoj was interviewed for *The Generosity Project* in November 2018.

Manoj's story reads like a modern-day version of Jesus' parable of the rich fool—that story in Luke 12 about the man who has everything, but who at the very height of his prosperity and self-satisfaction is called to account by God, and loses all that he holds dear.

It's an old and familiar story. It's one we all know, even if our experience of it is not as extreme as Manoj's. It's the story of the universal human impulse to take and take and take all the good gifts of God and hoard them for ourselves, only to discover—sooner or later—that it is a foolish and futile path. It is the story of greed.

Greed is the corruption of good human desire. Desire is a normal and good part of our experience. We see something good (or perhaps think about something good), and we are attracted to it. We want to embrace and enjoy its goodness. We desire it.

This is how God has made us as humans—to see and love and desire the good things he has created. But it's not meant to end simply with desiring, obtaining and enjoying the good things God has made. God's intention is that we not only enjoy the good things he gives, and thank and praise him as the Giver, but that we use them to bless others around us with goodness.

This is because the good things of the world are not just randomly thrown about the place by God in a giant heap. There is an *order* to them. Each one of them has a nature and purpose that is connected with other things. So, for example, ice-cream is good for eating, but not so good for washing your hair with. Playing games is good, but human life is a higher good—so playing an enjoyable game with your kids that threatened their lives would be a tragic misunderstanding of the ordering of the good things in the world.

At the centre of all that is good is God, the source and giver of every good thing. This is why to love God with all your heart, soul, mind and strength is the first and greatest commandment, because he is the greatest good, the good we should delight in and seek and love above all others. And the second great commandment shows that humanity too is to be loved. Next to loving God, loving your neighbour as yourself is our greatest duty (see Mark 12:31).

Greed is a stunted, corrupted, disobedient form of human desire. Rather than responding to the good things God gives by loving and thanking and praising God the Giver, the greedy person thinks only of the gift, and ends up loving and serving only himself.

What is more, rather than using and directing the good things God gives towards other people to love and bless them with goodness, greed selfishly clutches the good thing to itself, and seeks to do good only to itself. Moore Theological College Lecturer Dan Wu puts it like this:

> **What you have is this beautiful relationship of love and faithfulness between God and us, and us and each other, that just rebounds and grows and fills the world.**

That's how the world is meant to work; that's how we're meant to work. And that's why greed is such a dangerous and serious sin, because greed short-circuits this process. Instead of receiving and then reflecting and returning God's gifts, we receive them but then try and terminate the process on ourselves—we hold them in for ourselves rather than using them for the good of others.

Martin Luther once described sin as "the heart curved in on itself". And I think greed ties right into this. Greed is human desire turned back in on itself, and the result is ugly.

I remember when I was a kid, we had pizza for dinner one night, and then the next day I got home first from school. In the fridge were three pieces left over for afternoon tea—one for me, and one each for my two brothers. So what did I do? I got all three pieces out, chucked them in the microwave, and then took a huge bite out of each piece. But by then I was full, so I threw the rest in the bin.

Why did I do that?! It just makes no sense. The only possible answer is greed. I just wanted it all for myself. But the sad thing is, it mucked up and twisted and destroyed everything. I didn't enjoy the pizza—I got a tummy ache after three bites. My brothers, when they got home, were rightly angry at me and we fought. And the pizza itself got wasted and chucked in the bin.

This is a trivial and childish example, but when I think about my adult experience and those times

> where I know I've been greedy, things actually don't change that much. And when you look across the world and you see how greed destroys people and families and societies, you realize it's actually a really dangerous thing.
>
> And that makes sense, because greed is the absolute denial of the purpose for which we are created—and that is to give ourselves in love and faithfulness to others and to God.

The heart of the human problem, someone once said, is the problem of the human heart. The human heart bends inwards. It focuses on "carrying out the desires of the body and the mind" (Eph 2:3). Greed is just one very prominent, very ugly form of this impulse, as John Stevens says:

> Paul says in Ephesians that our greed is idolatry. We worship things rather than worshiping God, and we expect them to bring us benefits and salvation. We expect them to produce our identity, so we take our sense of self from what it is that we own. We look to them to give us security and to protect us from all the problems that there might be in the world. That may be ill health, or retirement, or an economic threat. We look to them to give us our liberty.

Like all forms of sin and false worship, greed does not deliver on its promise. In fact, it corrupts and destroys our humanity, hurts and damages others, and brings us under the righteous anger and judgement of God.

Greed is an ultimately destructive symptom of our self-directed, self-focused, self-loving hearts.

This makes what God has done through Jesus Christ all the more extraordinary. In Jesus, God has given a generous gift beyond all expectation, beyond all obligation. It's a gift so lavish and undeserved that we describe it not simply as generosity but as 'grace'—as a totally unmerited gift that is not only beyond the worthiness of the receiver, but is given *despite* the character of the receiver. Vaughan Roberts explains it like this:

> Christ is God's greatest gift. You could not have a greater gift than the gift of Christ, and the gift was not simply that Christ was born. That would be an amazing gift in itself—that Christ could leave all the glory of heaven to come to be born in the misery and the sin of this fallen world. But God gave him not just to be born, but to die. And he did it out of infinite love.
>
> The Bible tells us that God is a God of absolute holiness. He loves what is right. He hates what is evil, and must punish it. He's the God of justice, but he's also the God of great love. He longs to forgive us, longs to have relationship with us. The question is: how? How can the demands of his justice and his love both be met?
>
> Only through the cross of Christ—because when Jesus died, he satisfied the righteousness, the holiness, the justice of God as he took the penalty for sin. He died not for his own sin—he'd done nothing wrong—but for the sin of others. And then because

of his sacrifice, he's able to give us what we certainly don't deserve: the gift of relationship with God. Peter says in the Bible: "Christ also suffered once for sins, the righteous for the unrighteous, that he might bring us to God".[2]

What an amazing gift! See, where does Jesus belong? In heaven, on a throne, surrounded by angels worshipping him. Where does he end up? On earth, on a cross, surrounded by enemies jeering him. And he did it out of love for you and me.

That changes everything. Spiritual wealth is showered upon us. The moment we trust in Christ, we're in the right with God. We're his friends forever. We've got a certain hope. It changes our status before God, but much more than that, the Holy Spirit changes us internally as he massages these gospel truths deeper and deeper into our hearts. The result is inner transformation, and so people who are by nature inward-looking selfish takers are turned more and more outwards to God and to others as loving givers. That's the impact of our generous God's change in our lives through the greatest gift that's ever been given, the gift of Christ dying for us.

We might wonder whether the sheer outlandishness of God's generosity to us in Christ would leave us embarrassed, bashful, almost unwilling to accept such a gift

2   1 Peter 3:18

so far beyond what we deserve. But the response that God himself wants from us, and works within us by his Spirit, is a repentant, thankful, rejoicing trust in this extraordinary gift, and a transformed life that is no longer inwardly curved, but now looks upward to God and outward to others.

This is a liberation. We've been set free from the prison of our own self-regard and from all the destructive consequences that flow from it. The generous grace of God liberates us to be different people—people of lavish generosity rather than greed.

We'll look further at what the liberated, lavishly generous life looks like in part 3. But let's conclude this section by returning to Manoj's story, which by the grace of God didn't end like the story of the rich fool. With his business in tatters, and his son in a coma from which he was not expected to wake, Manoj became aware of something bigger than himself:

> What was resonating for me and my wife was the fact that there was a Christian couple praying for my son—and the woman in particular had wept bitterly for my son. I couldn't get my head around the concept of why a couple that I hardly knew would express so much compassion and love. They prayed for my son, and they got the church to pray as well.
>
> And on the fourth day of the coma, as the doctor approached my son's bed, my son suddenly bolted upright in bed like he had nothing wrong with him, and

started to pull away at all the wires.

You've got to realize: I was a very ruthless business-man, arrogant; I lived a very, very sinful life, in many, many ways, and didn't have any time for God. I mean, money was my God. But I remember turning to my wife and saying, "I am going to go to church. I am going to thank that couple. We're not going to their home. We are going to go to their church because they prayed for us. We are going to thank them and we are going to thank their God."

But I wasn't expecting to be in church a few weeks later, and to feel drawn to go back to church again after that. And I heard the message of the gospel, that Jesus Christ died for sinners like me. And I found myself, shortly after that, giving my life to the One who gave his life for me.

What it means for us

(Talk about one or more of the following questions together.)

1. What insight from the 'Input' section struck you most? Why?

2. "The heart of the human problem is the problem of the human heart." Where do you see this in your own life? Where do you see it in the lives of those around you or in society?

3. If money is like a god that the greedy heart worships, what does your own use of money reveal about your heart?

4. How would you describe your own experience of the grace of God in Jesus Christ?

5. If you have time, watch a real world story that relates to part 2 at thegenerosityproject.com, and talk about it together.

Give thanks and pray about what you've learned in part 2. As you pray, ask for God's help to change in the areas of struggle that you've considered.

Going further

- For more real world stories about how God's generosity transforms us, go to thegenerosityproject.com.
- If you haven't done so already, read the text or watch the video in the 'Input' section (above) sometime over the next few days. It will help solidify the ideas in your mind, as you continue to think and pray about generosity.

PART 3: A new, generous life

In part 2, we saw what a radically generous God we serve—a God who saves us from our selfishness and greed through the death and resurrection of his Son; a God who kindly sets us free to live a new life of love and generosity to others.

But what does that generous life look like?

Let's start by reflecting on what Scripture says about this new life.

Read and reflect: Set free to be generous

1. Think of a time when you've benefitted from someone else's kindness or generosity in a way that did
   not directly involve money. What are the things you
   remember most about this experience? How was it a
   blessing to you?

2. Read the following passage from Philippians:

   [1] So if there is any encouragement in Christ, any
   comfort from love, any participation in the Spirit,
   any affection and sympathy, [2] complete my joy by
   being of the same mind, having the same love,
   being in full accord and of one mind. [3] Do nothing
   from selfish ambition or conceit, but in humility
   count others more significant than yourselves.
   [4] Let each of you look not only to his own interests,
   but also to the interests of others. [5] Have this mind
   among yourselves, which is yours in Christ Jesus,

⁶ who, though he was in the form of God, did not count equality with God a thing to be grasped, ⁷ but emptied himself, by taking the form of a servant, being born in the likeness of men. ⁸ And being found in human form, he humbled himself by becoming obedient to the point of death, even death on a cross. (Phil 2:1-8)

a. What principle for generous Christian living does Paul lay down in this passage (especially in verses 3-4)?

b. How is this principle connected to the 'generosity' that Jesus showed?

3. Read this passage from Galatians. How are we to use the freedom we've received in Christ?

[13] For you were called to freedom, brothers. Only do not use your freedom as an opportunity for the flesh, but through love serve one another. [14] For the whole law is fulfilled in one word: "You shall love your neighbour as yourself." [15] But if you bite and devour one another, watch out that you are not consumed by one another. (Gal 5:13-15)

4. Now look quickly through the following passages. What area(s) of life does each one address, and in what ways are we encouraged to be loving and generous in those areas?

   a. 1 Corinthians 12:4-7

   > [4] Now there are varieties of gifts, but the same Spirit; [5] and there are varieties of service, but the same Lord; [6] and there are varieties of activities, but it is the same God who empowers them all in everyone. [7] To each is given the manifestation of the Spirit for the common good.

b. Matthew 5:43-45

[43] "You have heard that it was said, 'You shall love your neighbour and hate your enemy.' [44] But I say to you, Love your enemies and pray for those who persecute you, [45] so that you may be sons of your Father who is in heaven. For he makes his sun rise on the evil and on the good, and sends rain on the just and on the unjust."

c. Luke 14:12-14

[12] He said also to the man who had invited him, "When you give a dinner or a banquet, do not invite your friends or your brothers or your relatives or rich neighbours, lest they also invite you in return and you be repaid. [13] But when you give a feast, invite the poor, the crippled, the lame, the blind, [14] and you will be blessed, because they cannot repay you. For you will be repaid at the resurrection of the just."

d. 1 John 3:16-18

  [16] By this we know love, that he laid down his
  life for us, and we ought to lay down our lives
  for the brothers. [17] But if anyone has the world's
  goods and sees his brother in need, yet closes
  his heart against him, how does God's love
  abide in him? [18] Little children, let us not love in
  word or talk but in deed and in truth.

e. Colossians 3:12-14

  [12] Put on then, as God's chosen ones, holy and
  beloved, compassionate hearts, kindness,
  humility, meekness, and patience, [13] bearing
  with one another and, if one has a complaint
  against another, forgiving each other; as the

Lord has forgiven you, so you also must forgive. [14] And above all these put on love, which binds everything together in perfect harmony.

f. 1 Thessalonians 5:15

[15] See that no one repays anyone evil for evil, but always seek to do good to one another and to everyone.

Input: A new generous life

(Watch video 3 or read the following section.)

The Pharisees are the obvious bad guys of the Gospels. They're always opposing Jesus, and Jesus sends some stinging put-downs in their direction. (When was the last time you heard a Christian call someone else a 'serpent', a 'blind fool' or a 'whitewashed tomb'? Those are only some of the things that Jesus calls the Pharisees in Matthew 23 alone.)

But we often don't realize that the Pharisees were extremely upright and moral people, or at least appeared to be. The Pharisees saw themselves as being foremost among God's saved people, Israel. And they were! God had given Israel the law to obey, and the Pharisees' approach to obeying God's law was to break it down into an achievable series of boxes that they could tick. Keep the ceremonial and food laws—check. Worship at temple and go to synagogue—check. Tithe from everything, including the herbs in the window box—check. And they did all this diligently.

In fact, their approach to the godly life was disturbingly like that of some Christian people today. After being saved through the death of Jesus and given eternal life, some Christians see the Christian life as a matter of ticking certain boxes. Obey the ten commandments—check. Worship at church and go to Bible study—check.

Put some money in the plate—check. And generally don't do anything too heinous—check. For some Christians, the godly life is about obeying the rules and keeping your nose clean.

Now, this approach mightn't make you a serpent or a blind fool—the diligent law-keeping of the Pharisees was a hypocritical mask for an unconverted, rebellious heart. But if we think that the Christian life is largely about obeying commands and not doing anything wrong, then we have failed to notice something vital—in fact, *central*—in the teaching of Jesus.

According to Jesus, the whole point of the Old Testament law, and of all the commandments, was to teach Israel to *love*; to love God and to love their neighbour (Matt 22:36-40). When Jesus commanded his disciples, "just as I have loved you, you also are to love one another" (John 13:34), it was a new commandment because it had a new motive and a new model—Jesus' own sacrificial love for his people. But it was not an out-of-the-blue commandment (see 1 John 2:7). 'Love' was exactly what the Old Testament law had always been about. Paul makes this clear in Romans 13:

> Owe no one anything, except to love each other,
> for the one who loves another has fulfilled the law.
> For the commandments, "You shall not commit
> adultery, You shall not murder, You shall not steal,
> You shall not covet," and any other commandment,

are summed up in this word: "You shall love your neighbour as yourself." Love does no wrong to a neighbour; therefore love is the fulfilling of the law. (Rom 13:8-10)

The commandments are like shorthand guides or rules of thumb, but they all aim at the over-arching goal of love. A faith-grounded, hope-filled love is the basic form of the Christian life—a love that doesn't try to minimize our response to God's salvation by ticking boxes, but rather reaches out in constant generosity and grace to others.

As Tim Clemens says, this is the point of one of Jesus' most famous parables:

> A man comes to Jesus and says, "Who is my neighbour?" This guy knows that he is supposed to love his neighbour as himself, but he's wondering, "How do I satisfy this command? Who do I have to love?"
>
> Jesus' response is to tell a story, the parable of the Good Samaritan, which basically corrects the question. And the answer is effectively this: "Don't ask, 'Who is my neighbour?', but, 'Who can I be a neighbour to?'" In other words, don't ask, "Who do I have to love?" Ask, "Who can I love?"
>
> And so, again and again, the principle is love, not law. As Christian people, we're not sitting there, asking in every situation, "What are the minimum obligations I have to meet in order to be accepted by God?" No—now we ask, "How can I maximize my opportunities to love

people, since I have been loved and accepted by God?" That's going to look different in all sorts of circumstances and areas. But as a general principle, it's going to be about renouncing self-interest, and the pursuit of pleasure and success, and seeking instead to be creatively generous where I can be. It means looking for opportunities to put others forward, and lift them up.

What the Spirit of God does through the gospel of Jesus Christ is to redirect our selfish, inwardly curved hearts. He turns our hearts radically outwards—to love and serve God as our Creator and Saviour and Lord, and to love and serve our neighbours as ourselves. As Dan Wu puts it:

Love should be our goal in life. So whenever we interact with someone, our first thought should be, "How can I do good to you in the way God has done good to me?" And generosity is a key aspect of that sort of love.

Generosity really is a readiness to give beyond what is expected or deserved. It's really a delight in bringing delight to others. And that's why I think the Bible talks so much about money and how we use it. Money moves so quickly and can be used so easily to do good to another person. And so we should use our money generously for the good of others.

But money is only one form of currency that God has given into our lives. There are many other valuable commodities that God gives us that we can spend for other people, such as our expertise or experience, or our care and hospitality. But I think most pressingly in our society, which is so rushed and hyperactive, one of the most valuable commodities we can generously give to others is our unhurried time and attention.

Many of us have a budget for our money. We think about how much we have, how much we can give, and what we'd like to use it for. Wouldn't it be great if we applied that same sort of thinking to all the other valuable commodities God has given us in our lives to give generously in love to others? How can we use all the different gifts God has given us to love others generously?

John Stevens makes a similar point:

In our Western culture where people are very busy, time is often the most difficult thing for people to be able to give. We need to be generous with our time. We can also be generous with the spiritual gifts that God has given us to be used in the service of the church and to help advance the gospel. We can be generous with the energy that we have, and the emotional energy that we have, so as to serve others. We can also be generous with the *opportunities* that we have—we live in particular places; we have been given particular networks of relationships. God wants us to use those generously to serve others and to serve the gospel.

We are to be generous in using *everything* that God has blessed us with to serve others and to build others up. That's what it means to live in love.

God calls us in the gospel to abandon our lives to the service of others; to lay down our lives for one another, as Christ laid down his life for us. This is the Christian life. It's so much more than ticking boxes or avoiding breaking the rules. It's the radically generous, big-hearted life that we were created to live, modelled on the character of the generous God who made us in his image and who now makes this new life possible through the liberating, sacrificial love of Christ shown on the cross.

What it means for us

(Talk about one or more of the following questions together.)

1. What insight in the 'Input' section struck you most? Why?

2. What do you find hardest or most challenging about the gospel's call to be radically generous?

3. *(If you watched video 3)* Did you identify with any of the stories shared on the video? Which ones, and why?

4. Look back at your answers in question 4 in the 'Read and reflect' section. Pick at least one or two areas of life in which you have a particular opportunity to be generous in some way. If you're part of a group, discuss these opportunities with one another and talk about what practical steps you could take to be generous in these areas.

5. Think of a time when you were able to show generosity to someone else. In what ways were you blessed by the opportunity to be generous? Where have you seen the truth of Jesus' teaching that "it is more blessed to give than to receive" (Acts 20:35)?

Give thanks and pray about the things you've learned in part 3. Pray particularly that God would enable you to be generous in the areas of life you've considered.

Going further

- For more real world stories about how God's generosity transforms us, go to thegenerosityproject.com.
- If you haven't done so already, read the text or watch the video in the 'Input' section (above) sometime over the next few days. It will help solidify the ideas in your mind, as you continue to think and pray about generosity.

PART 4: Money and the new life

At various points in our exploration of generosity so far, we've touched on money—as a classic expression of the attitudes of the heart, either in selfishness or in generosity.

How should we define 'money'? As Tim Clemens put it back in part 1, money is basically a liquid form of God's provision for us: it enables us to gain and to use the good things of God's creation. Money is therefore one of God's good and generous gifts to us, but it is a very potent gift. By accumulating it, we store up power for ourselves— power to get things, or to do things. We build security for ourselves and gain influence over others.

It's time for us to think specifically about money, and how it fits into what we have learned about generosity. As we'll see, money has great potential, and we can use money fruitfully in the service of God and of others. But in a fallen world filled with corrupt hearts like ours, money also has its downside.

Read and reflect: Danger, faithfulness and generosity

1. What do the following verses say about the dangers and limitations of money?

   a. Proverbs 11:4

      ⁴ Riches do not profit in the day of wrath,
      but righteousness delivers from death.

   b. Proverbs 11:28

      ²⁸ Whoever trusts in his riches will fall,
      but the righteous will flourish like a green
      leaf.

c. Proverbs 16:16

> [16] How much better to get wisdom than gold!
>> To get understanding is to be chosen rather
>> than silver.

d. Proverbs 23:4-5

> [4] Do not toil to acquire wealth;
>> be discerning enough to desist.
> [5] When your eyes light on it, it is gone,
>> for suddenly it sprouts wings,
>> flying like an eagle toward heaven.

2. Read the following verses from 1 Timothy:

^{6} But godliness with contentment is great gain, ^{7} for we brought nothing into the world, and we cannot take anything out of the world. ^{8} But if we have food and clothing, with these we will be content. ^{9} But those who desire to be rich fall into temptation, into a snare, into many senseless and harmful desires that plunge people into ruin and destruction. ^{10} For the love of money is a root of all kinds of evils. It is through this craving that some have wandered away from the faith and pierced themselves with many pangs. (1 Tim 6:6-10)

^{17} As for the rich in this present age, charge them not to be haughty, nor to set their hopes on the uncertainty of riches, but on God, who richly provides us with everything to enjoy. ^{18} They are to do good, to be rich in good works, to be generous and ready to share, ^{19} thus storing up treasure for themselves as a good foundation for the future, so that they may take hold of that which is truly life. (1 Tim 6:17-19)

What are the particular dangers facing those who:

a. desire to be rich?

b. are already "rich in this present age"?

3. Part of the upside of money is that it can be put to good uses; for example, in faithfully meeting responsibilities we might have. What area(s) of life do each of the following verses address, and what does the faithful use of money look like in those areas?

a. 2 Thessalonians 3:10-12

> [10] For even when we were with you, we would give you this command: If anyone is not willing to work, let him not eat. [11] For we hear that some among you walk in idleness, not busy at

work, but busybodies. [12] Now such persons we command and encourage in the Lord Jesus Christ to do their work quietly and to earn their own living.

b. Romans 13:1-7

[1] Let every person be subject to the governing authorities. For there is no authority except from God, and those that exist have been instituted by God. [2] Therefore whoever resists the authorities resists what God has appointed, and those who resist will incur judgement. [3] For rulers are not a terror to good conduct, but to bad. Would you have no fear of the one who is in authority? Then do what is good, and you will receive his approval, [4] for he is God's servant for your good. But if you do wrong, be afraid, for he does not bear the sword in vain. For he is the servant of God, an avenger who carries out God's wrath on the wrongdoer. [5] Therefore

one must be in subjection, not only to avoid God's wrath but also for the sake of conscience. [6] For because of this you also pay taxes, for the authorities are ministers of God, attending to this very thing. [7] Pay to all what is owed to them: taxes to whom taxes are owed, revenue to whom revenue is owed, respect to whom respect is owed, honour to whom honour is owed.

c. 1 Timothy 5:8

[8] But if anyone does not provide for his relatives, and especially for members of his household, he has denied the faith and is worse than an unbeliever.

d. 1 Timothy 5:17-18

> [17] Let the elders who rule well be considered worthy of double honour, especially those who labour in preaching and teaching. [18] For the Scripture says, "You shall not muzzle an ox when it treads out the grain," and, "The labourer deserves his wages."

4. Using money well is not only about being faithful in paying our bills. As we've already seen above, money is also a gift that we can use generously with others. In the following verses, what generous *actions* are encouraged, and what *motives* (if any) exist for doing them?

a. Deuteronomy 15:7-11

> [7] "If among you, one of your brothers should become poor, in any of your towns within your land that the LORD your God is giving you, you shall not harden your heart or shut your hand against your poor brother, [8] but you shall open your hand to him and lend him sufficient for his need, whatever it may be. [9] Take care lest there be an unworthy thought in your heart and you say, 'The seventh year, the year of release

is near,' and your eye look grudgingly on your poor brother, and you give him nothing, and he cry to the LORD against you, and you be guilty of sin. [10] You shall give to him freely, and your heart shall not be grudging when you give to him, because for this the LORD your God will bless you in all your work and in all that you undertake. [11] For there will never cease to be poor in the land. Therefore I command you, 'You shall open wide your hand to your brother, to the needy and to the poor, in your land.'"

b. Mark 12:41-44

[41] And he sat down opposite the treasury and watched the people putting money into the offering box. Many rich people put in large sums. [42] And a poor widow came and put in two small copper coins, which make a penny. [43] And he called his disciples to him and said to them, "Truly, I say to you, this poor widow has put in more than all those who are contributing to the offering box. [44] For they all contributed out of their abundance, but she out of her poverty has put in everything she had, all she had to live on."

c. Proverbs 14:31

[31] Whoever oppresses a poor man insults his
    Maker,
  but he who is generous to the needy
    honours him.

d. Acts 20:33-35

[33] "I coveted no one's silver or gold or apparel.
[34] You yourselves know that these hands
ministered to my necessities and to those who
were with me. [35] In all things I have shown you
that by working hard in this way we must help
the weak and remember the words of the Lord
Jesus, how he himself said, 'It is more blessed to
give than to receive.'"

Input: The downside and upside of money

(Watch video 4 or read the following section.)

When I was a child, I understood money in terms of milk bottles.

'Milk bottles' were my favourite lolly—a small, vanilla-flavoured, milk-bottle shaped treat that we used to buy at the kiosk after swimming, or at the tuckshop at school, in the days when school tuckshops had not been swept clean of all foods containing sugar or fat.

Milk bottles cost one cent each. And so when the princely sum of 20 cents came into the possession of my six-year-old self, I knew what I was really holding in my sweaty little palm: 20 milk bottles!

What $10 meant I could barely comprehend, let alone $100. When such unheard-of riches swam before my eyes, I pictured myself swimming and gorging myself in a great vat of milk bottles beyond counting.

What my greedy little brain had already grasped was that money is power—the power to have and to use the good things of this world, and in particular for *me* to have them.

This is why the Bible has something of a love-hate relationship with money. It is often seen in the Bible as a good gift from God to be received and used with thanksgiving, because it signifies and represents the good gifts of creation that God has so generously given us. When the people all donate money for the building of the temple, Solomon understands that all they are doing is really giving back to God what has come from him anyway: "But who am I, and what is my people, that we should be able thus to offer willingly? For all things come from you, and of your own have we given you" (1 Chr 29:14). In Proverbs, wealth and riches are seen to be the good consequences of a wise, God-fearing life (e.g. Prov 22:4).

But in Proverbs, and throughout Scripture, money is also seen as a false, temporary and dangerous object of trust. The one who trusts in riches (Prov 11:28) or runs after wealth (Prov 23:4) will be disappointed. Money and wealth are good gifts, but make terrible masters.

We've already seen this in Manoj's story in part 2— how greed and the love of money enslaved him and almost destroyed him, but how God's lavish generosity in the gospel set him free. And we've also considered how greed is a distortion of the good purposes God has for us and his world. As Dan Wu put it in part 2:

> **What you have is this beautiful relationship of love and faithfulness between God and us, and us and each other, that just rebounds and grows and fills the world. That's how the world is meant to work; that's how we're meant to work. And that's why greed is such a dangerous and serious sin, because greed short-circuits this process. Instead of receiving and then reflecting and returning God's gifts, we receive them but then try and terminate the process on ourselves—we hold**

them in for ourselves rather than using them for the good of others.

The two positive words that Dan highlights—'love' and 'faithfulness'—ring like bells throughout the Scriptures, describing not only God's character, but also what our character should be as we receive and then rightly employ the good gifts God gives. Vaughan Roberts takes up the story:

> **There are two words the Old Testament uses again and again when it tries to describe the character of God: faithfulness and love. And when the Lord Jesus Christ came to earth, John says, "We have seen his glory, glory as of the only Son from the Father, full of grace and truth".[1] The same qualities: grace (love) and truth (faithfulness).**
>
> **Now that we've been called to belong to God, and are his children, we are to bear the family likeness. We too should be marked by faithfulness and love in absolutely every area of our lives, including how we handle our money.**

Using our money with love—that is, with grace and generosity to others—is the focus of this book, but before we think further about that, it is worth thinking briefly about what it means to deal with money *faithfully*. Vaughan Roberts again:

1   John 1:14

We should be people of absolute faithfulness; absolute integrity. That means always dealing honestly, including with money. It means keeping our word, even when it's very costly, including financially costly. And it means always fulfilling our responsibilities.

The Bible gives us various responsibilities for our money, and they begin at home. So the first responsibility is to ensure we provide for ourselves and our families, including our parents when they get older. We're very aware of people living longer these days—and so for many of us, fulfilling our responsibility to our parents may be very costly indeed, in terms of time, energy and money.

Then there's what we owe to the state; to governing authorities. The Bible says we owe those in authority our respect, and we should pay our taxes. Jesus said, "Render to Caesar the things that are Caesar's".[2]

But there's also an obligation we have within our church family: to support those who are set apart for gospel ministry. Most people go out to work to earn a living, to earn a wage, to get food on the table and so on. People like me (pastors) don't do that. We're set apart to give ourselves wholly to the work of the gospel, and we are only able to do that because church members are fulfilling their responsibility to support the ministry of word and prayer that pastors are undertaking.

2   Mark 12:17

This final point about our responsibility to support those who labour among us in gospel work is not the usual way we think about giving at church. We tend to see the money we give as an expression of our generosity, for which the pastors should be truly thankful. And this is partly true. It can be very generous, and pastors are (almost) always thankful.

However, it's striking that when Paul talks about people giving money to pay for gospel work among them, he speaks of wages being earned—about how even an ox that treads out the grain receives its due reward (1 Cor 9:6-10). He concludes, "In the same way, the Lord commanded that those who proclaim the gospel should get their living by the gospel" (1 Cor 9:14; cf. 1 Tim 5:17-18).

If a pastor or elder is working in our congregation, supporting him financially is not really an act of generosity—because remember, generosity is about kindly giving someone something unexpected, or beyond what is deserved or earned. It's not generosity on the part of our boss to pay our wages each week; nor is it generosity for a congregation to pay money to support its pastors.

And yet as important as it is to be *faithful* with our money, it's vitally important that we also be *generous*— that we use our money as part of the new life of love to which the gospel calls us. As we've already seen, God sets us free from our inwardly curved hearts and our self-regard to be radically generous people. Generosity means going beyond our responsibilities to bless others generously with everything we have, including our money. Tim Clemens says:

> God sets us free to start thinking about how we can generously use our money for the growth of the gospel, both at our own churches and beyond that. Rather than just thinking, "How do I maintain things and meet my obligations?" I can start thinking, "How can I invest to see real gospel growth through my generosity?"
>
> And if that sounds hard, it's important to remember that contentment and generosity go hand in hand. I don't mean that you should only start being generous once you're content, because it's often the other way around. Often it's the process of being generous that helps us become more content people—because generosity is an antidote to our natural tight-fistedness, and our natural desire for more and more.
>
> What I mean is this: rather than thinking to yourself, "Should I forego X or Y so that I can give that money away and be generous?" instead start by being faithful in your responsibilities, and then look around and ask: "How can I be extravagantly, ferociously generous here?"
>
> And you may well find that having been generous, you don't really worry any more about that money that you could have spent on other things. So be faithful, be generous, and most likely your lifestyle will start to come in line.

This way of thinking about being faithful and generous with our money is completely counter-cultural. From an early age, we're taught to think about money in quite the opposite sort of way: firstly, as a means of getting what we want for ourselves; secondly, as a resource that we reluctantly have to use up in meeting our various responsibilities; and only then, with whatever is left over, as a means of bringing blessing to others through generosity.

But the gospel of Christ turns all that on its head. First, be honest, faithful and true in meeting your various obligations and responsibilities; then, be radically generous to contribute to the material and spiritual needs of others; and then enjoy whatever is left over, with contentment and thanksgiving to God who gives so many good gifts.

The gospel of Jesus also overturns worldly motives and standards for being generous with money. In our world, people often give very publicly and noticeably in order to be praised for their generosity (like the hypocrites Jesus criticizes)—but gospel generosity is quiet and unobtrusive, so that our left hand doesn't know what our right hand is doing (Matt 6:2-4). In our world, we are hugely impressed when some billionaire gives away massive sums to charity, but Jesus teaches that generosity is a matter of the heart, not the amount. The poor widow of Mark 12 gave away the last two small coins she had left, and in so doing gave far more than all the rich people who were making big donations out of their abundance (Mark 12:41-44). The cost to the *giver* reveals the true value of the gift to God, because it reveals a generous heart that has been transformed by the gospel.

What it means for us

(Talk about one or more of the following questions together.)

1. What insight from the 'Input' section struck you most? Why?

2. How are you going with using your money faithfully and meeting financial responsibilities? Are there any specific areas where you need to make a change?

3. How are you going with using your money (and thinking about your money) in a way that cultivates trust in God and contentment? In what specific areas might you be tempted to lack contentment and to slip into something like 'covetousness'?

4. Paul told Timothy to charge "the rich in this present age" to "be rich in good works [and] to be generous and ready to share" (1 Tim 6:17-18). Brainstorm some ways in which you can be rich in good works, generous, and ready to share.

Give thanks and pray about the things you've learned in part 4. Pray particularly that God would enable you to be generous in the areas of life you've considered.

Going further

- For more real world stories about how God's generosity transforms us, go to thegenerosityproject.com
- If you haven't done so already, read the text or watch the video in the 'Input' section (above) sometime over the next few days. It will help solidify the ideas in your mind, as you continue to think and pray about generosity.

PART 5: The partnership of the generous

Read and reflect: The grace of giving

1. Read the following passages from 2 Corinthians:

   [1] We want you to know, brothers, about the grace of God that has been given among the churches of Macedonia, [2] for in a severe test of affliction, their abundance of joy and their extreme poverty have overflowed in a wealth of generosity on their part. [3] For they gave according to their means, as I can testify, and beyond their means, of their own accord, [4] begging us earnestly for the favour of taking part in the relief of the saints—[5] and this, not as we expected, but they gave themselves first to the Lord and then by the will of God to us. [6] Accordingly, we urged Titus that as he had started, so he should complete among you this act of grace. [7] But as you excel in everything—in faith,

in speech, in knowledge, in all earnestness, and in our love for you—see that you excel in this act of grace also.

⁸ I say this not as a command, but to prove by the earnestness of others that your love also is genuine. ⁹ For you know the grace of our Lord Jesus Christ, that though he was rich, yet for your sake he became poor, so that you by his poverty might become rich. ¹⁰ And in this matter I give my judgement: this benefits you, who a year ago started not only to do this work but also to desire to do it. ¹¹ So now finish doing it as well, so that your readiness in desiring it may be matched by your completing it out of what you have. ¹² For if the readiness is there, it is acceptable according to what a person has, not according to what he does not have. ¹³ For I do not mean that others should be eased and you burdened, but that as a matter of fairness ¹⁴ your abundance at the present time should supply their need, so that their abundance may supply your need, that there may be fairness. ¹⁵ As it is written, "Whoever gathered much had nothing left over, and whoever gathered little had no lack." (2 Cor 8:1-15)

⁶ The point is this: whoever sows sparingly will also reap sparingly, and whoever sows bountifully will also reap bountifully. ⁷ Each one must give as he

has decided in his heart, not reluctantly or under compulsion, for God loves a cheerful giver. [8] And God is able to make all grace abound to you, so that having all sufficiency in all things at all times, you may abound in every good work. [9] As it is written,

> "He has distributed freely, he has given to the
> poor;
> his righteousness endures forever."

[10] He who supplies seed to the sower and bread for food will supply and multiply your seed for sowing and increase the harvest of your righteousness. [11] You will be enriched in every way to be generous in every way, which through us will produce thanksgiving to God. (2 Cor 9:6-11)

a. In 2 Corinthians 8:1-5, Paul uses the churches of Macedonia as an object lesson in generosity. Which features of their generosity do you find most striking, and why?

b. From both of these passages, what are the right motivations and attitudes for generous giving?

c. How should the amount of giving be determined?

d. How does God bless those who give? Why does God bless those who give?

The shape of Christian generosity

The heartbeat of the radical generosity that Paul talks about in 2 Corinthians 8-9 is the gospel of Jesus—the one who was rich beyond all splendour, yet became poor so that we through his poverty might become rich.

But the gospel is not only the key motivation for generosity; it also shapes the *direction* of Christian generosity. It helps us to decide where and how to be generous. We see this particularly in Paul's letter to the Philippians.

As you read the following sections from Philippians, underline anything that describes the kind of 'partnership' (or 'fellowship' or 'sharing') Paul had with the Philippians:

> [3] I thank my God in all my remembrance of you, [4] always in every prayer of mine for you all making my prayer with joy, [5] because of your partnership in the gospel from the first day until now. [6] And I am sure of this, that he who began a good work in you will bring it to completion at the day of Jesus Christ. [7] It is right for me to feel this way about you all, because I hold you in my heart, for you are all partakers with me of grace, both in my imprisonment and in the defence and confirmation of the gospel. (Phil 1:3-7)

> [29] For it has been granted to you that for the sake of Christ you should not only believe in him but also suffer for his sake, [30] engaged in the same conflict

that you saw I had and now hear that I still have. (Phil 1:29-30)

¹⁹ I hope in the Lord Jesus to send Timothy to you soon, so that I too may be cheered by news of you. ²⁰ For I have no-one like him, who will be genuinely concerned for your welfare. ²¹ For they all seek their own interests, not those of Jesus Christ. ²² But you know Timothy's proven worth, how as a son with a father he has served with me in the gospel. ²³ I hope therefore to send him just as soon as I see how it will go with me, ²⁴ and I trust in the Lord that shortly I myself will come also.

²⁵ I have thought it necessary to send to you Epaphroditus my brother and fellow worker and fellow soldier, and your messenger and minister to my need, ²⁶ for he has been longing for you all and has been distressed because you heard that he was ill. ²⁷ Indeed he was ill, near to death. But God had mercy on him, and not only on him but on me also, lest I should have sorrow upon sorrow. ²⁸ I am the more eager to send him, therefore, that you may rejoice at seeing him again, and that I may be less anxious. ²⁹ So receive him in the Lord with all joy, and honour such men, ³⁰ for he nearly died for the work of Christ, risking his life to complete what was lacking in your service to me. (Phil 2:19-30)

[1] Therefore, my brothers, whom I love and long for, my joy and crown, stand firm thus in the Lord, my beloved. (Phil 4:1)

[10] I rejoiced in the Lord greatly that now at length you have revived your concern for me. You were indeed concerned for me, but you had no opportunity. [11] Not that I am speaking of being in need, for I have learned in whatever situation I am to be content. [12] I know how to be brought low, and I know how to abound. In any and every circumstance, I have learned the secret of facing plenty and hunger, abundance and need. [13] I can do all things through him who strengthens me.

[14] Yet it was kind of you to share my trouble. [15] And you Philippians yourselves know that in the beginning of the gospel, when I left Macedonia, no church entered into partnership with me in giving and receiving, except you only. [16] Even in Thessalonica you sent me help for my needs once and again. [17] Not that I seek the gift, but I seek the fruit that increases to your credit. [18] I have received full payment, and more. I am well supplied, having received from Epaphroditus the gifts you sent, a fragrant offering, a sacrifice acceptable and pleasing to God. [19] And my God will supply every need of yours according to his riches in glory in Christ Jesus. [20] To our God and Father be glory forever and ever. Amen. (Phil 4:10-20)

2. What did Paul and the Philippians share or have partnership in? How did the Philippians express their partnership with Paul?

3. How did Paul respond to the 'partnership' shown by the Philippians?

4. How did God respond?

Input: Generosity and gospel partnership

(Watch video 5 or read the following section.)

The extraordinary passages from 2 Corinthians 8-9 that we reflected on above are, in many ways, very like this book: they are unavoidably about giving away our money, but they are also about so much more than that. They're about how the gospel of Christ changes people to their very core.

There are two groups of people in these passages: the Macedonian Christians whom Paul is citing as a striking example of generosity, and the Corinthian Christians to whom he is writing.

Paul had a complicated relationship with the Corinthians. He loved them deeply, but they were a difficult bunch, with all sorts of issues in their church life: factionalism, immorality, arrogance, and more. And as he deals with all these problems throughout his letters to them (the letters we call 1 and 2 Corinthians), Paul keeps pointing them repeatedly to the one thing that should shape and direct everything they do: the cross of Jesus Christ. For Paul, the cross provides the reason for everything, and the standard by which everything is judged. The cross is why factionalism is ridiculous, and why immorality can't be tolerated, and why arrogance is so totally out of place for Christ's people. Paul wants the Corinthians to live a cross-shaped life, as indeed his own ministry is a cross-shaped one.

That's also why he points them to the example of the Macedonian Christians. Though they were living in 'extreme poverty', they begged for the privilege of being part of the relief effort for their fellow believers in Jerusalem. They longed to be like the crucified Christ, who gave away his very life for the sake of others. Jason Roach puts it like this:

> God isn't just a God of faithfulness; he's a God of love and generosity too. And if I'm looking for one verse that puts that really succinctly it's probably 2 Corinthians 8:9: "For you know the grace of our Lord Jesus Christ, that though he was rich, yet for your sake he became poor, so that you by his poverty might become rich".
>
> It's a beautiful verse that speaks of how Jesus left the palace of heaven and became nothing so that we might enjoy his spiritual riches. And that not only gives us the forgiveness that we need to be friends with God, but it also transforms our hearts to be generous people, following in the footsteps of the Lord Jesus Christ himself.

The Macedonian example is remarkable. But it's just the kind of thing that cross-shaped people do—that is, people who have grasped that laying down your life for the sake of others (like Jesus did) is what the Christian life is actually about.

Could there be anything more radical in our money-obsessed 21st-century Western society than this kind of self-forgetful, extravagant generosity? Could there be any more powerful way to declare to our neighbours that we follow a crucified saviour? Dan Wu summarizes the challenge of 2 Corinthians 8-9 like this:

> Not many of the people doing *The Generosity Project* could describe themselves as living in extreme poverty, or any poverty really. Most of us are wealthier than pretty much any generation that has lived.
>
> And yet more often than not we give begrudgingly. Only after we've taken care of everything we want to do, and if there's anything left over, do we think about giving.
>
> But really, the Macedonians reversed the normal priority. Rather than asking, "How much do my wants require, after which I can think about giving to you", they asked first, "How much do your needs require before I think about fulfilling my wants?"

The Macedonians, in their extreme poverty, were driven by the gospel to this new life of extravagant generosity. How much more should those of us living in comparative wealth be driven by the gospel to do the same?

However, the gospel not only drives us to be extravagantly generous; it also shapes *where that generosity might be directed*. And it does this not by giving us a formula, or a ranked list of priorities, but by inviting us to be part of the extraordinary thing that God is doing in our world. Vaughan Roberts explains it this way:

When we think about the most significant things happening in the world today, our minds might go to the huge political issues that are being discussed in Washington or London or Beijing, or we might think of those news items that are flashed on the bulletins. But actually the most significant thing that's going on in the world is almost never mentioned in any news bulletin, and that is God's great work of spreading the gospel to the ends of the earth.

As the gospel is proclaimed by the Holy Spirit, God is calling people into his kingdom that they might know the living God. And by the same Spirit, through the gospel, he's transforming people into the likeness of the Lord Jesus. He's calling and preparing a people for eternity, because one day Jesus will return. And when he returns, there will be the great division. And sadly, those who continue in rebellion against God will be separated from his presence for all eternity.

So there's nothing more significant than the work of the gospel around the world. And wonderfully, we can be part of that great work. In his grace, he not only calls us to know him, but calls us to be involved in gospel ministry.

St Paul in Philippians frequently describes Christians as partners in the gospel. In 1 Corinthians, Paul describes himself and his colleagues as fellow workers in God's service. I think that's one of the most astonishing things in the Bible—that people like us can be partners and fellow workers with God. It's awesome.

When we grasp that God has called us to be partners with him—and each other—in the great gospel enterprise, it really does change everything. It transforms our understanding, not just of money and generosity, but of everything we do.

For example, when we serve in some way at church—say by volunteering to help lead the children's program—we're not just 'volunteering' or 'going on a roster'. We're working as partners in the gospel. We're investing the resources God has given us—in this case, our time, our words, our experience, our energy—into advancing the gospel cause of seeing people come to know God through Christ and grow to be like Christ in their lives.

When you read the Bible with a Christian friend, you're being a partner in the gospel. When you share a word of challenge or encouragement with a non-Christian friend, you're being a partner in the gospel. And when you give to support your own local church or some other gospel ministry, you're using the financial resources God has given you to be an investment partner in God's gospel work in the world.

This gospel-partner perspective changes the way we think about using our money, in at least three important ways.

First, it helps us think quite differently about the money we contribute at church. It is indeed true, as we noted in part 4, that Christians have an obligation to support the pastors and elders and overseers that labour among us in gospel ministry. But we should never regard that obligation as a drag or a burden, because in using our money to support our pastors, *we're partnering with them—and with God—in the work of the gospel that is happening in and through our church.* We're investing in what God himself is actively doing in our little part of the world—which is why we will also be glad to give generously to the ministry of our church, above and beyond what is required to support the current pastoral staff. We will want to see the work of the gospel not just supported and paid for, but constantly expanding and growing in our midst. We will be delighted to give generously to hire new staff, to start new ministries, or to build new infrastructure, because there's no better way to invest the money that God has generously allowed us to accumulate than to be generous with it in the partnership of the gospel.

Second, it casts a whole new light on those many Christian causes and ministries that seek our support beyond the local church. Here's what a friend in student ministry recently wrote about the awkward business of asking Christians to donate to his ministry:

> Christians like me in self-funded ministries can fall into the trap of feeling like we're a drain on the Christian community, like we're just going to people cap in hand and saying, "Can I have some money please?" But what we're doing is so much bigger than that. Christians in self-funded gospel ministries who ask for financial support are, in effect, saying to people: "Will

you partner with me, and with God himself, in the work of the gospel? Will you invest your worldly wealth in something that will last for eternity?" The very act of asking people to support gospel ministry—whether or not people are actually able to support you—is a blessing to them, because you're asking them to walk by faith, not by sight; to fix their eyes not on what is seen and temporary, but on what is unseen and eternal; to invest in the kingdom that is eternal; to become a partner in the extraordinary work God is doing in our world.

Whether we're on the asking or being-asked side of supporting gospel ministry—and many of us will be on both sides at different times—this gospel-partnership perspective allows us to be open, honest and guilt-free. We can ask our brothers and sisters to give money or time or some other resource, knowing that in doing so we are offering something wonderful—the opportunity to be a partner in the life-changing work that God is doing in our world. And when we receive such an offer, we can respond positively and with gratitude, even when our answer is no: "Thank you so much for blessing me with this chance to be a gospel partner with you, but my funds are fully committed to other gospel work at the moment."

Finally, this gospel-partnership perspective provides us with a fresh way of thinking about where to give our money away, among the overwhelming needs and opportunities that confront us in our world. We all have a natural human tendency to respond to the needs that confront us the most urgently or loudly—whether in a media campaign about poverty in a developing country, or from a friend in ministry who asks for our help. And it is a privilege to respond joyfully and spontaneously to these needs (as we noted above). However, the perspective of the gospel and its growth in the world provides us with a framework to think carefully and intentionally about where we will direct our generosity. We may well choose to give to a gospel cause that is not high profile, is not run by a friend of ours, and is not banging urgently on our door for funds—because we consider that this ministry has enormous value or potential for the growth of the gospel.

A final word from Tim Clemens:

> As Christians, we've got to be driven by the principle of love. What does it mean to love people? It means meeting their needs. If someone has physical needs, what does it look like to meet those needs? Well, you do what you can to provide food and shelter. But, if someone has spiritual needs, how do you meet them? Well, you share the life-giving message of Jesus with them. As Christian people, we need to be about loving people in both deed and word, in caring for both the body and the spirit. We can't separate them too much. Yet, it would be a mistake to say that they're of the same importance.
>
> I think that the most important form of ministry we can offer to people is evangelism. As Tim Keller says,

that's not because the spiritual is more important than the physical; it's because the eternal is more important than the temporal.[1] Those in physical poverty need our love and care here and now, and we should give it. But their eternal spiritual destiny is more important than their current physical poverty.

So I would be very hesitant to tell someone, "No, no, don't give to a secular charity; just give to Christian causes"—because if the secular charity is caring for the poor and looking after people, that's a great thing. If you can support it, by all means do so.

At the same time, there's a bunch of non-Christian people who will support that charity as well. With very few exceptions, a non-Christian is not going to support the work of a local church or Christian ministries or mission agencies. Yet, those Christian ministries are the very ones that seek in love to meet people's spiritual and eternal needs.

So just practically, I would always advise someone, "Do what you can to care for people's spiritual and physical needs, but consider prioritizing their eternal needs over their temporal needs." That might look like choosing to support your local church and Christian mission organizations as a first priority before you give yourself to supporting Christian charities, or non-Christian charities.

---

1   T Keller, 'The Gospel and the Poor', *Themelios,* vol. 33, no. 3, December 2008, pp. 8-22. Available online: themelios.thegospelcoalition.org/article/the-gospel-and-the-poor.

What it means for us

(Talk about one or more of the following questions together.)

1. What insight in the 'Input' section struck you most? Why?

2. Why do you think it's important to God that we are not just givers, but cheerful givers? Based on what you've seen throughout this project, what steps can you take to cultivate a growing attitude of cheerful giving?

3. Do you know of Christians who are in particular 'need', compared to your relative 'abundance' (2 Cor 8:13-15)? What, if anything, can you do to help meet their need?

4. In what ways does the notion of 'partnership' help to expand your horizons on contributing to a range of gospel ministries?

5. Think about some specific Christian ministries or organizations that you value. How are you expressing your partnership with these ministries? Are there any new ways in which you're able to be generous?

6. In light of what we've seen in this study, how would you assess your current patterns of giving and generosity?

Give thanks and pray about the things you've learned in part 5. Pray particularly that God would enable you to think and act genuinely and practically in light of what you've learned.

Going further

- For more real world stories about how God's generosity transforms us, go to thegenerosityproject.com.
- If you haven't done so already, read the text or watch the video in the 'Input' section (above) sometime over the next few days. It will help solidify the ideas in your mind, as you continue to think and pray about generosity.

Preparing for part 6

The sixth and final part of *The Generosity Project* looks both back and forward—back at what we have learned about generosity, and forward to what we are going to do about it. To make the most of this, spend 30 minutes on your own thinking through the following questions before you begin part 6.

1. Think back over parts 1-5. If you had to name one or two key truths or ideas that have particularly challenged, surprised, encouraged or helped you in your personal thinking about generosity, what would they be?

2. It's easy to work through material like this but then never get around to putting the ideas into practice. Think and pray through the following five steps of a personal action plan on generosity, and write down some points to share with others.

Step 1: Where?

Think of one area of life where God is currently giving you a new opportunity to be generous (e.g. a particular relationship, a specific way of serving in your local church, a ministry that would benefit from your financial partnership).

Step 2: What?

Think of (at least) one specific way in which you can show generosity in this situation. What practical steps would you need to take to put this into action?

Step 3: When?
Develop a timeframe for putting your plan into action. When will you take action? Will this be an ongoing situation, or are you thinking of a one-off act of generosity? Be specific about developing a timeframe and a plan (if appropriate).

Step 4: How?
Start to consider some specifics of what generosity might look like in this situation (you might have started doing this as part of step 2 or step 3). For example, if you're considering financial partnership in a gospel ministry, how much might you give, and how often? If you're considering giving time to a particular ministry or organisation, what will this look like?

Step 5: Pray

Finish the process by committing your plans to God. For example, ask him to shape your plans and to bring them to fruition. Pray that your act of generosity would be a great blessing to others, and to you. Pray that God would give you a spirit of humility and cheerfulness as you put this plan into action. Praise God for his grace and generosity to you.

PART 6: Reflection, action and prayer

It may seem like we're getting to the end of *The Generosity Project*. But of course it can't be the end, if all that we've been learning about generosity is true.

To live a radically generous, big-hearted life is a lifelong project. It is launched by God's amazing generosity to us in the gospel, and sustained and grown in us by God's Spirit. It's a life of repentance and faith; of turning away from our selfish and greedy past, putting our trust in the generous God who redeems us, and then beginning a new life that no longer turns inward on ourselves but flows out to others in grace and generosity in a thousand different ways. It's a life lived in the fellowship of God's people, who work shoulder-to-shoulder in the 'partnership of the generous', and who keep spurring each other on to grow in generosity.

In this final part of *The Generosity Project*, we're going to look back over what we've learned, and look forward to the practical difference this refreshed understanding of generosity is going to make in our lives.

Let's begin by looking back.

Reflect: Insights and questions

1. Look back through the insights that struck you in the 'What it means for us' section of parts 1-5 of *The Generosity Project*. What do you think has changed in your understanding of generosity?

2. What questions do you still have about generosity and what it would look like in your life?

3. Read the following verses from James and pray for each other to be doers of the word, and not hearers only:

   [22] But be doers of the word, and not hearers only, deceiving yourselves. [23] For if anyone is a hearer of the word and not a doer, he is like a man who looks intently at his natural face in a mirror. [24] For he looks at himself and goes away and at once forgets what he was like. [25] But the one who looks into the perfect law, the law of liberty, and perseveres, being no hearer who forgets but a doer who acts, he will be blessed in his doing. (Jas 1:22-25)

Input: From principle to practice

(Watch video 6 or read the following section.)

Thinking back over the five parts of *The Generosity Project* so far, what are the key lessons or principles that have emerged from our study of what the Bible says about generosity? We could summarize them like this:

1. Our whole world is built on generosity. God created us and everything not because he needed to, or was obligated to, but from the generous out-flowing of his goodness. This is what generosity really is: kindly and graciously giving someone more than you're obliged or expected to give. And this is not only what God has done in creating everything that exists, but what he continues to do in sustaining and providing for his creation. The right response to all generosity—and most especially God's generosity—is basically twofold: a response of trust, thanksgiving and praise to the one who is being generous; and an answering desire to be generous ourselves with the things we have been given.

2. However, the human impulse is not towards generosity but selfishness. We aren't thankful and generous by nature. In fact, quite the reverse—the natural orientation of our hearts is not outwards to others in love and generosity, but inwards towards our own interests and purposes. Our bad attitudes to money and material possessions—greed, self-

sufficiency, pride, dishonesty and corruption—all stem from our rebellious, inwardly curved hearts. But God, in his most extravagant act of generosity, provides salvation, healing and freedom for our sinful hearts. By the death and resurrection of Jesus, he wipes our hearts clean, and sets us on a new path of love and generosity towards others.

3. The work of God's Spirit through the gospel of Jesus sets us free to live new lives of joyful love and generosity. This radically generous life is by no means just about money. It is expressed in every aspect of our lives: in open-hearted hospitality, in using our personal abilities to serve others in church or in the community, in devoting our time and attention to the needs of others, in being forbearing and forgiving of the sins and shortcomings of others, in wrestling in prayer for others, and much more.

4. Generosity is about more than money, but money is a key aspect of the generous life. Money is a potent gift from God that represents the power to have things and to use things. And this 'having and using' can be directed inwards to our own greedy ends, or outwards to others in faithfulness and generosity. We should employ our money *faithfully* (in meeting our various responsibilities, such as to family and church), and *generously* (in helping those in need, and in furthering the work of the gospel in our church and further afield).

5. Financial generosity, like everything in the Christian life, is driven by the gospel that has set us free to be generous. This means that our generosity should not be random, or determined just by the loudest voice appealing for our help. Our partnership in the great cause of the gospel—with God, with one another, and with Christians all over the world—should shape our priorities and decisions about where and how to be generous.

What does all this mean in practice—not just immediately, but for the months and years to come? That's something to talk honestly about together (see the 'Planning for action' section on page 126), but here are four nuggets of practical advice to inform your discussion.

a. Prayerful planning

For many of us, a lack of generosity in our lives is simply due to thoughtlessness. We get caught up in the whirl of daily life and activity, and our resources (financial and otherwise) seem to disappear before our eyes. We find ourselves lacking in generosity because the gifts we could be generous with—our time, our skills, our financial and other resources—seem to be fully accounted for, without us knowing exactly why.

The antidote to this is prayerful planning—to ask for God's help in refocusing our priorities and spending habits, and then to prepare a budget for our time and money.

Where are my resources currently going? What responsibilities do I need to meet with faithfulness? What opportunities are there for generosity, particularly in gospel partnership? And then what is left over for other things?

The famous preacher John Wesley became, through his writings and ministry, a very wealthy man. But as his income steadily increased, he resolved to increase not his standard of living, but his 'standard of giving':

> ...in 1731 Wesley began to limit his expenses so he would have more money to give to the poor. He records that one year his income was £30, and his living expenses £28, so he had £2 to give away. The next year his income doubled, but he still lived on £28 and gave £32 away. In the third year his income jumped to £90, again he lived on £28, giving £62 away. The fourth year he made £120, lived again on £28 and gave £92 to the poor.
>
> Wesley... believed that with increasing income, the Christian's standard of giving should increase, not his standard of living. He began this practice at Oxford and he continued it throughout his life. Even when his income rose into the thousands of pounds, he lived simply and quickly gave his surplus money away.[1]

---

1   CE White, 'Four Lessons on Money from One of the World's Richest Preachers', *Christian History*, vol. VII, no. 3, issue 19, 1988.

The details of Wesley's circumstances and decisions were his own, and are not meant to serve as a rule for us to follow. But his example is a sober challenge to our attitudes. When our income is far in excess of what is required to meet our needs and responsibilities, how do we think about that excess? As an opportunity for a higher standard of living, or an opportunity to bless others with the abundance God has given us?

What is particularly relevant in Wesley's example is the fact that he thought about this *in advance*. He determined what he was going to do with his money before it came—and so was primed and ready to be generous.

In biblical terms, he was 'prudent'. He considered the future with a wise discernment, and resolved to act accordingly. Prudence can refer to the decisions we make today or this week, or to our planning for the coming year. Many people—including many Christians—don't stop to take account of their income and expenses, and to think about their priorities for the coming year, including where and how they are going to express generosity. One important practical outcome of *The Generosity Project* could simply be putting some time aside in our calendars to take stock, to pray, and to plan how we are going to be more faithful and generous in the year to come.

b. Spontaneity and joy

This emphasis on prudence and thoughtful planning should not lead us to think that practical generosity is a joyless, spreadsheet kind of affair. God loves a cheerful giver, after all. And very often, God will bring random opportunities for generosity across our path. John Stevens comments:

> Although it's important to be intentional and to plan our giving, we also need to be able to respond spontaneously to other needs, and to make sure that we have the capacity to be able to do that. It may well be, for example, a world disaster and we feel moved to respond. It may be that we hear about the persecution of Christians in a part of the world, and we want to give to help support them. It may be our neighbours are in need in some particular way or a member of our church has a need that we had not anticipated, or it may be a gospel opportunity that comes across our path. Maybe a mission that's being conducted. Maybe a gospel worker who we hear is in need. We shouldn't plan all of our giving so that we have no capacity to respond to the spontaneous opportunities that come our way.

It's wise to plan for spontaneity—to have some margin in our lives and budgets to respond generously to needs that come across our paths.

And as we start to be more generous, whether in a planned or spontaneous way, the apprehension or fear we might have about giving away our money begins to dissolve. Vaughan Roberts puts it like this:

> Someone once said to me, "You're only really giving when it costs you something". And that can be quite a scary thing to do. And so I often encourage people, "Just do it". It can be a scary thing before you do. You're nervous about it. "Will I be left short if I give this money away?"
>
> But once you've done it, then you get a taste and you realize that God is faithful. Assuming we haven't been rash or thoughtless, God provides for our needs, and equips us to keep on being generous. More and more what I'm praying for is that people will discover the joy of giving—but that only happens once we start doing it.

c. How much?

You may have noticed that up to this point we've studiously avoided the question that Christians often ask first with respect to generosity: *How much should I give?* We've mainly done this because it is not the first or best question to ask. Once we've worked out what generosity really is, and how Christ sets us free to be radically generous people, then the 'how much' question recedes into the background somewhat. Instead of "How much *should* I give?" we find ourselves joyfully asking, "How much *can* I give?"

All the same, the 'how much' question often troubles Christians, particularly with respect to 'tithing'—the common practice in Christian history of putting aside the first tenth of your income to give back to God (for the work of the church and the gospel). Should Christian generosity be expressed in tithing? And is that pre-tax or after tax?

We don't have space here to discuss this issue in full, and godly, Bible-believing Christians have different views about how binding the 10% tithing figure is on Christians. All the same, some important things can be said:

- Understanding tithing means understanding how Old Testament laws apply to Christians today (tithing is an Old Testament practice; it is not mentioned in the New Testament). Christians are not under the law of Moses in the way that Old Testament Israel was. We live on this side of the fulfilment of all God's promises in Christ. However, the Old Testament law still plays an important part in the Christian life—in fact, the apostle Paul says that the Old Testament was really written for *us*, on whom the end of the ages has come, to teach and warn and encourage us to lead a new life of godliness in response to God's salvation in Christ (see 1 Cor 10:1-13; Rom 15:1-4).

- So what do the Old Testament tithing laws teach us today? First of all, we need to recognize that tithing, or putting aside the first tenth (Lev 27:30-33), was only one part of the way Israel was to respond to God's generosity. They were also to give the 'first fruits' (whether animals or crops) to the Lord (e.g. Deut 15:19-20), as well as giving other contributions and offerings at different times (e.g. Deut 12:5-7). The principle behind these various tithes and offerings was that Israel should respond to the grace and generosity of God by joyfully giving back to him the first and best part of what they had—not because God needed it, but so that they would never forget his grace and provision.

- We have already seen in *The Generosity Project* that this is also how the New Testament thinks about generosity—as a glad response to God's generosity to us. In fact, we have been given *even more grace* in the Lord Jesus Christ than Israel could ever have imagined, and so to limit our giving to just a tenth would seem a meagre response.

- Perhaps this is the best way to apply the concept of tithing to our 'how much' question—as an encouragement and a challenge to our pattern of generosity. For some of us, putting the first 10% of our income aside for church and for generosity would be a shock to our financial system—it would highlight our lack of faithfulness towards our church's ministry, or our meagre generosity for the growth of the gospel. For many of us, 10% would be a low bar of generosity in terms of how much excess we have (of income over expenses), and how many opportunities exist for us to be generous. If we are giving away less than 10%, we should stop and seriously consider whether we have good reasons for doing so (and perhaps we may). But if tithing is not particularly difficult for us to achieve, let us be eager for the privilege (like the Macedonians in 2 Corinthians 8) of joyfully going far beyond 10%.

d. Keep talking

One of the main purposes of *The Generosity Project* has simply been to drag the topic of generosity out into the light of day. As Vaughan Roberts put it in part 1:

> I think one big problem people have with generosity is that it's a great unmentionable. We don't tend to talk about money, and we don't tend to talk about giving. I'd love us to break that taboo, because the Bible is not at all embarrassed to talk about these things and nor should we be.

Hopefully, the experience of reading, thinking, studying, discussing and praying about money and giving over the past several weeks has begun to break that taboo, and has made generosity a topic that we feel comfortable to talk openly about.

But it would be an obvious mistake to *stop* talking about generosity, now that we've got the conversation started, and for a very simple reason. The impulse that inclines us to put generosity in the cupboard and not talk about it is still very much with us, because it's an aspect of our sinful focus on self. If we don't keep talking about generosity, and encouraging one another to be generous, we will very quickly revert to our default state—which is to consign generosity once more to the 'great unmentionable' category, and get on with our lives and our spending as if generosity were not a key facet of the Christian life.

This is also why this book is a 'project'—it's something for us to work on *together*, because we very much need each other. The writer to the Hebrews urged his readers to "exhort one another every day, as long as it is called 'today', that none of you may be hardened by the deceitfulness of sin" (Heb 3:13); and to "consider how to stir up one another to love and good works" (Heb 10:24).

Like the rest of the Christian life, generosity is a team sport. God graciously gives us each other, to encourage, exhort, remind, comfort, admonish and support each other. Now that we've started talking about generosity, let's not stop.

Planning for action

At the end of part 5, as part of the preparation for this final session, you should have put some thought into a personal action plan. Break into pairs or threes, and share your plans with each other, praying that God would help you to see the opportunities clearly and to be cheerful givers in whatever areas you're seeking to be generous in.

Step 1: Where?

Think of one area of life where God is currently giving you a new opportunity to be generous (e.g. a particular relationship, a specific way of serving in your local church, a ministry that would benefit from your financial partnership).

Step 2: What?

Think of (at least) one specific way in which you can show generosity in this situation. What practical steps will you need to take to put this into action?

Step 3: When?

Develop a timeframe for putting your plan into action. When will you take action? Will this be an ongoing situation, or are you thinking of a one-off act of generosity? Be specific about developing a timeframe and a plan (if appropriate).

Step 4: How?

Start to consider some specifics of what generosity might look like in this situation (you might have started doing this as part of step 2 or step 3). For example, if you're considering financial partnership in a gospel ministry, how much might you give, and how often? If you're considering giving time to a particular ministry or organisation, what will this look like?

Step 5: Pray

Finish the process by committing your plans to God together. For example, ask him to shape your plans and to bring them to fruition. Pray that your act of generosity would be a great blessing to others, and to you. Pray that God would give you a spirit of humility and cheerfulness as you put this plan into action. Praise God for his grace and generosity to you.

Next steps

Come back together as a group. Talk together about how you might encourage one another over the weeks and months ahead to put your plans into action, to look for more opportunities for generosity, and to look for opportunities to encourage others with the things you've learned from doing *The Generosity Project*. You might decide to revisit the subject in (say) three months' and six months' time to see how your various plans and actions are unfolding, and how what you've learned has had an impact in your Christian life.

Conclude by giving thanks again to God for all his generous grace, and praying that we might respond with thanksgiving and generosity of our own.

❂matthiasmedia

Matthias Media is an evangelical publishing ministry that seeks to persuade all Christians of the truth of God's purposes in Jesus Christ as revealed in the Bible, and equip them with high-quality resources, so that by the work of the Holy Spirit they will:

- abandon their lives to the honour and service of Christ in daily holiness and decision-making
- pray constantly in Christ's name for the fruitfulness and growth of his gospel
- speak the Bible's life-changing word whenever and however they can—in the home, in the world and in the fellowship of his people.

Our resources range from Bible studies and books through to training courses, audio sermons and children's Sunday School material. To find out more, and to access samples and free downloads, visit our website:

www.matthiasmedia.com

How to buy our resources

1. Direct from us over the internet:
   – in the US: www.matthiasmedia.com
   – in Australia: www.matthiasmedia.com.au

2. Direct from us by phone: please visit our website for current phone contact information.

3. Through a range of outlets in various parts of the world. Visit **www.matthiasmedia.com/contact** for details about recommended retailers in your part of the world.

4. Trade enquiries can be addressed to:
   – in the US and Canada: sales@matthiasmedia.com
   – in Australia and the rest of the world: sales@matthiasmedia.com.au

Register at our website for our **free** regular email update to receive information about the latest new resources, **exclusive special offers**, and free articles to help you grow in your Christian life and ministry.

Also by Geoff Robson

Thank God for Bedtime

What God says about our sleep and why it matters more than you think

Sleep. It seems an unlikely topic for a Christian book, doesn't it?

Yet we all need to sleep, and we spend a fair proportion of our lives doing just that (or, for some of us, *trying* to do just that).

What's more, when we carefully read the Bible we discover that God actually cares about our sleep and has quite a bit to say about it.

In this engaging, practical, and strikingly gospel-centred book, Geoff Robson offers a 'theology of sleep' that is full of wise and helpful Christian insights for all of us.

Also by Tony Payne

The Thing Is

God, you and your purpose in life

"The thing is."

That's what we say when we are at last getting to the point.

The bushes have been beaten around, the chase has been cut to, and we are finally getting to the thing we've been avoiding but that now needs to be spoken.

What is that thing for you?

What is the thing that makes sense of your life but that you don't often talk about?

What is the point of it all, the purpose, the real reason you get out of bed in the morning?

From the author of *The Trellis and the Vine* comes an opportunity to pause and take stock of our lives, and to discover the life-changing purpose that God has for each one of us.

FOR MORE INFORMATION OR TO ORDER CONTACT:

Matthias Media
Email: sales@matthiasmedia.com.au
www.matthiasmedia.com.au

Matthias Media (USA)
Email: sales@matthiasmedia.com
www.matthiasmedia.com

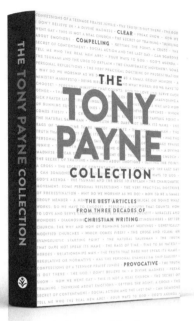